OCT 1 7 2014

BUILT FOR SUCCESS

THE STORY OF

MTV

Published by Creative Education
P.O. Box 227, Mankato, Minnesota 56002
Creative Education is an imprint of The Creative Company
www.thecreativecompany.us

DESIGN BY **ZENO DESIGN**
PRODUCTION BY **CHELSEY LUTHER**
ART DIRECTION BY **RITA MARSHALL**
Printed in the United States of America

PHOTOGRAPHS BY Alamy (Jeff Greenberg, NASA Archive),
Dreamstime (Dan Talson), Getty Images (Don Arnold/
WireImage, David Becker/WireImage, L. Cohen/WireImage, Fin
Costello/Redferns, Justin de Villeneuve, Ian Dickson/Redferns,
Gerry Goodstein/NBC/NBCU, Handout, Jeff Kravitz/FilmMagic,
Frank Micelotta, Frank Micelotta/ImageDirect, Christopher
Polk, Mario Ruiz/Time Life Pictures, Time & Life Pictures, Rob
Verhorst/Redferns), Newscom (Johns Pkl/Splash News, Dave
Longendyke/ZUMAPRESS, HELENE SELIGMAN/AFP)

LIBRARY OF CONGRESS CATALOGING-IN-PUBLICATION DATA
Gilbert, Sara.
MTV / Sara Gilbert.
p. cm. — (Built for success)
Summary: A look at the origins, leaders, growth, and innova-
tions of MTV, the music video channel founded in 1981, which
is one of cable television's leading entertainment channels
today.
Includes bibliographical references and index.
ISBN 978-1-60818-395-1
1. MTV Networks—History—Juvenile literature. I. Title.

PN1992.8.M87G55 2014
791.45'611—dc23   2013029616

CCSS: RI.5.1, 2, 3, 8; RH.6-8.4, 5, 6, 8

First Edition
9 8 7 6 5 4 3 2 1

BUILT FOR SUCCESS

THE STORY OF

MTV

SARA GILBERT

At exactly 12:01 A.M. on August 1, 1981, a 6-word announcement ushered in a new cable television station designed to broadcast music videos 24 hours a day, 7 days a week: "Ladies and gentlemen, rock and roll." As those words were spoken, a video clip of the launch of the space shuttle *Columbia* was shown on the screen, followed by footage of the historic Apollo 11 moon landing in 1969. But instead of hoisting an American flag on the surface of the moon, the astronaut proudly planted a flag featuring the logo of the new network: MTV, an abbreviation for Music Television. After that introduction, the new network aired the appropriately named "Video Killed the Radio Star" by a band called the Buggles.

CHAPTER ONE

A Vision for Videos

I n 1979, *Billboard*, a magazine devoted to covering the music industry, held the first-ever Video Music Conference in Los Angeles, California. Although videos had been made for songs in one form or another since the 1930s and '40s, the **medium** was just beginning to be used seriously by rock and roll musicians, and videos by such popular artists as Blondie, David Bowie, and Rod Stewart were previewed at the conference.

One of the people at that conference was John Lack, a 33-year-old **executive** with the cable television company Warner-Amex Satellite Entertainment Company. Lack, self-described as a "major rock 'n' roller," was part of a panel discussion entitled "Video Music—Tomorrow is Here Today." During that presentation, he announced his plan to launch a 24-hour music video network that would highlight the top musicians and songs of the day.

Although Lack's boss, Jack Schneider, supported the idea, the record companies weren't sure that it was a good plan—or that they should provide the videos that would be aired on the new channel. Lack and Schneider also had to secure

Superstar David Bowie experimented with musical styles and was known for his theatricality

funding from the **board of directors** at Warner-Amex, convince independent cable operators to carry the channel, and persuade businesses to advertise on it as well.

None of that was easy. Record companies were hesitant to provide videos to the new channel free of charge, as MTV had requested. The Warner-Amex board declined the original request for $25 million to start the station. And only a handful of cable operators was willing to take a chance on the unproven concept. But by January 1981, Lack's idea had gathered enough backers to receive the requested funding from Warner-Amex.

To meet Lack's goal of being on-air by August 1, his small team of creative young executives, including a radio personality named Robert Pittman, had to work quickly. Once they had agreed on a name—officially Music Television, but known as MTV—they had to hire VJs, the television equivalents of radio disc jockeys (DJs), to announce the upcoming songs and interview musicians on the air. They then had to encourage more cable operators to add the channel to their offerings. And they had to prepare a 24-hour playlist with the fewer than 300 videos in existence at the time.

On the night of July 31, 1981, the MTV staffers took a bus from their headquarters in New York City to a bar in Fort Lee, New Jersey, the nearest city where the channel was being broadcast, to watch its **debut**. Although they all cheered wildly when "Video Killed the Radio Star" by the Buggles was played, the launch was far from flawless. "The first hour of MTV was a total, unmitigated disaster," Pittman admitted later. "Everything that could have gone wrong did go wrong."

Not only was the video selection limited (at least three Rod Stewart videos aired during that first hour), but the clips of the VJs introducing songs weren't paired with the correct videos. The audio was muffled, or completely silent, for many viewers. Media reviews universally panned the new network.

But when Pittman sent some of his crew out to gather reactions from local record stores, they were told that Buggles albums, which weren't played on the radio, were selling quite well, thanks to their exposure on MTV. Such an example

Rod Stewart (right) sang with Rolling Stones guitarist Ronnie Wood in the band Faces

of public acceptance helped MTV convince record company executives to start producing more, and better, videos, because the videos could in turn help them sell more albums. But the network was still encountering resistance from cable operators in many major markets, including New York and Los Angeles, that were unwilling to pay the fees necessary to add the network. To help persuade them to carry the channel, MTV launched an ad campaign in the spring of 1982 that featured famous musicians—including Mick Jagger, the lead singer of the Rolling Stones—saying, "I want my MTV."

The plan worked. People started calling their cable providers, begging them to carry MTV. By the time MTV celebrated its first birthday, it was on the air in most major markets, including New York. "It legitimized us," said Schneider. "People called their cable companies and said to the poor operators, in these lousy imitations of Mick Jagger, 'I want my MTV.'"

MTV spent $2 million on that ad campaign. A year later, it spent $250,000 to expand its reach even further by filming a **documentary** about Michael Jackson's almost 14-minute "Thriller" video and obtaining rights to air the video's world premiere. MTV had been accused of not showing videos that had been made by African American artists, because they didn't appeal enough to the mainstream television audience, and many young African Americans were not watching the channel. The "Thriller" premiere—and the heavy play the video received on MTV in the following months—gave them a reason to watch. The success of "Thriller" also helped the young network, which relied on advertisers for its income, to enjoy its first **profits**.

The "Thriller" phenomenon gave MTV the prominence it needed to host its next must-see event: the first-ever Video Music Awards (VMA), which aired on September 14, 1984. Although the awards given out were serious, including Video of the Year for The Cars hit "You Might Think," the tone of the awards show was much more irreverent than traditional shows, from the comedic banter of hosts Bette Midler and Dan Aykroyd to the live performance of "Like a Virgin" by Madonna. "It redefined music events on television," said longtime MTV executive John Sykes.

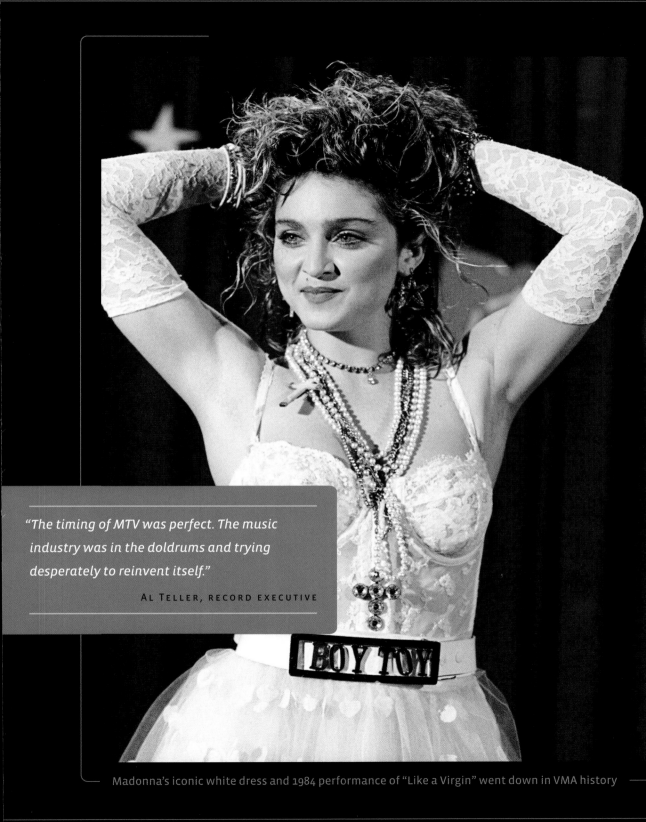

> "The timing of MTV was perfect. The music industry was in the doldrums and trying desperately to reinvent itself."
>
> AL TELLER, RECORD EXECUTIVE

Madonna's iconic white dress and 1984 performance of "Like a Virgin" went down in VMA history

The first name floated for MTV was The Music Channel. Founder Robert Pittman thought that it complemented The Movie Channel, which was run by the same company. When the rest of the team of executives rejected that name, Pittman assigned the task of naming the channel to them. Among that group was Steve Casey, a programming executive. He made a list of several names, including MTV—an abbreviation for Music Television. "I liked the way MTV looked when I doodled it," Casey said. "I said, 'Let's call it Music Television.'" When it became clear that none of the six other people in the group had a better idea, they agreed to accept Casey's suggestion for the time being. But they didn't love it. "Music Television became the final compromise," said Fred Seibert, the longtime head of program services. "Nobody liked it. We all hated the name MTV."

CHAPTER TWO

More than Music

By the following year, the young network found itself caught in the middle of an ownership squabble. Warner-Amex had decided that it wanted to sell some of its cable channels. MTV Networks—which included MTV and its sister station VH1 as well as kid-friendly Nickelodeon and part of the movie channel Showtime—was put up for sale.

The network's senior management, many of whom had been part of MTV since its founding, tried to put together enough cash to buy it themselves. Before they could finalize a deal, MTV Networks was sold to mass-media giant Viacom for $525 million in September 1985.

The sale stung many of MTV's executives who had poured their hearts and souls into developing the network, and several of them, including Pittman, left the company within two years. The new owners were more driven by a desire to make money than by a love of music, and they brought a more intense attitude to the previously fun-loving atmosphere of MTV. "It started to become about profit and programming," said Allen Newman, a **producer** who started his career at MTV in 1981 and worked there until 1987. "The attitude changed. The fun had gone out of it."

In the late 1980s, Sumner Redstone became the majority owner of Viacom—and MTV

The change in ownership also brought a new philosophy about programming. Suddenly, the network's commitment to airing videos or music-based shows 24 hours a day was in jeopardy. Ratings had slipped after peaking in 1983, and Viacom's leadership pushed MTV to find new programming that would bring in more viewers—and more advertisers. They wanted to see a dance show, a news show, and a game show worked into the regular schedule.

The few remaining members of the original MTV crew weren't happy about the new direction the channel was heading. But they also recognized that there were now more cable television options for the 18-to-25-year-olds who made up their target **market**, and they had to try something new to capture their attention. So they introduced *The Week in Rock*, a music news show, and the dance show *Club MTV*, the first program to be given a daily time slot on the network.

Club MTV, which was hosted by a flamboyant VJ known as "Downtown" Julie Brown, showed beautiful young men and women dancing to music performed by such **emerging** artists as Janet Jackson, Taylor Dayne, and Paula Abdul. It was a huge hit for MTV, and it helped launch careers for both the musicians and the dancers featured on it. Abdul, for example, was able to release a Top 40 album and eventually become a judge on the television show *American Idol*; one of the dancers was Camille Donatacci, who later married (and divorced) actor Kelsey Grammer and starred in *The Real Housewives of Beverly Hills*.

Although *Club MTV* was popular, it was *Remote Control*, a game show that quizzed contestants about television trivia, that truly established MTV as a popular-culture channel. *Remote Control* first aired on December 7, 1987. It featured comedians Ken Ober, Colin Quinn, Denis Leary, and Adam Sandler and was a huge success. But its launch was controversial within MTV. "Doing a game show on MTV was heresy," said Doug Herzog, the president of MTV Network Entertainment Group, who was the network's news director at the time. "Of the three new shows we started, *Remote Control* was the most transformative."

Club MTV VJ "Downtown" Julie Brown was remembered for her "Wubba Wubba Wubba" catchphrase

The launch of *Remote Control* proved to be a turning point for the network. Ratings improved, and advertising increased. Perhaps most significantly, however, it also marked a move toward an even more dramatic change in programming. Before 1988, every show had at least a slight connection to music—even *Remote Control*, which included questions about song lyrics and appearances by such artists as "Weird Al" Yankovic and LL Cool J. But then the network introduced *The Big Picture*, which was about movies, and the *Half Hour Comedy Hour*. Neither had anything to do with music.

MTV staffers worried that the success of such shows would lead future programming even farther away from music. Lee Masters, the general manager, sent out a memo explaining the new programming strategy and reassuring everyone that music would always be the network's base. "Is MTV moving away from music?" he wrote. "Absolutely not."

What MTV *was* edging away from was its comfort zone of Top 40 music. In 1985, it had dedicated a regular time slot to a heavy metal video show, which featured the loud, hard-driving music of such bands as Metallica and Twisted Sister. In 1986, it added *120 Minutes*, a late-night alternative music show that ran on the network for 14 years. And in 1988, it introduced *Yo! MTV Raps*, a weekly show highlighting the emerging hip-hop and rap **genre**.

Network executives had been nervous about venturing into rap. They didn't think it fit MTV's format or that there would be a big enough audience for it. They finally agreed to run a two-hour special on a Sunday afternoon to test the market. When that show became the most highly rated in MTV's history, executives gave the green light to a weekly, then a daily, show devoted to rap. As the 1990s began, *Yo! MTV Raps* became one of the most popular programs on MTV.

"At some point, the M in MTV changed from music to money."

NICK RHODES, KEYBOARDIST FOR DURAN DURAN

Yo! MTV Raps, co-created by Ted Demme (center), featured weekday hosts Ed Lover (left) and Doctor Dré

The Buggles' Geoff Downes and Trevor Horn

KILLING THE RADIO STARS

The Buggles wrote "Video Killed the Radio Star" in 1979, two years before MTV's first broadcast. The song was penned as a commentary on the changes coming, thanks to the emerging technology of the time. Home video recorders were just becoming popular, and musicians had started recording basic videos to accompany their songs. "We were excited about that," said Trevor Horn, one of the members of the band. "It felt like radio was the past and video was the future. There was a shift coming." Although the song wasn't a huge hit in the United States when it was released (reaching number 40 on the U.S. charts as compared with number 1 in the United Kingdom), it was the obvious choice for the first video to run on MTV. It was also the network's selection as its one-millionth video 18 years later, on February 27, 2000.

CHAPTER THREE

Breaking the Mold

MTV executives had been uncertain about rap, but they were downright adamant that **acoustic** music wouldn't be an appropriate fit for MTV. Once again, such a view was misguided. Thanks to a recent resurgence of interest in folk music, the barebones, personalized, instrumental approach of *MTV Unplugged*—which featured a musician sitting on a stool with a guitar or at a piano with a microphone, performing for a live audience—proved to be hugely successful when it was launched in 1989.

MTV Unplugged was closely tied to the network's founding principles and was able to feature musicians that its traditional audience appreciated, including Elton John, Aerosmith, and former Beatle Paul McCartney. It lacked the extravagance and pageantry for which MTV had become known—but in the midst of all the big-hair heavy metal videos and fast-paced hip-hop songs that had become popular on the channel, the simplicity of *MTV Unplugged* became its biggest appeal. Its success spawned similar shows on VH1 as well, including the popular *Storytellers* program in which artists told autobiographical stories during a live performance.

Paul McCartney remained one of the most successful composers and recording artists of all time

Most of the other new programming planned for MTV in the early- and mid-1990s, however, strayed from the network's musical roots. MTV ventured into fashion with *House of Style*, hosted by supermodel Cindy Crawford, in 1989. It jumped into politics with the *Choose or Lose* series during the 1992 U.S. presidential campaign. That same year, it launched the MTV Movie Awards and aired a talk show called *You Wrote It, You Watch It* featuring a young comedian named Jon Stewart. In 1993, the animated show *Beavis and Butt-head* debuted.

Some of those shows were more successful than others. *Choose or Lose* was considered by many to have been critical in getting young voters interested in the presidential candidates, and it was the first in a series of politically themed shows that followed. *Beavis and Butt-head* enjoyed eight seasons of popularity with young teenage "misfits" around the country who saw bits of themselves in the two title characters. But *You Wrote It, You Watch It*, in which viewers sent in funny stories to be acted out on the show, was canceled after less than a year on the air.

The program that redefined MTV as more than "music television" was *The Real World*—one of the earliest reality shows and the model for the spate of "reality" programming that followed. *The Real World* was originally intended as a soap opera for teenagers. But traditional soap operas, which tell dramatic stories about a cast of characters over a long period of time, were expensive to produce. Paying professional actors, **scriptwriters**, costumers, and a crew to tape the show could cost more than $500,000 a week. One MTV staffer offered a creative solution to that problem: Create an unscripted show, in which average people would be the stars. The idea was to find a diverse group of young adults who would live together in a New York City apartment. A camera crew would follow them around, documenting the natural dramas occurring in their lives. "We pitched it at breakfast," said producer Jonathan Murray. "It was bought by lunch."

The first episode of *The Real World* was televised on May 21, 1992. It achieved

Presidential candidate Bill Clinton answered questions during a 1992 segment of *Choose or Lose*

a rating, or percentage of the television viewing audience, of 0.9—three times the ratings that the videos aired immediately before the show had received (0.3). Its new, unexpected format and the issues that came up over the course of each show appealed to a young audience. The cast members of *The Real World* tackled such topics as sexuality, substance abuse, and prejudice; in 1994, *The Real World: San Francisco* featured an openly gay man who died of HIV/AIDS just hours after the final episode aired.

The show's success surprised many of the longtime executives at MTV, some of whom had predicted that it would last for only one season. *The Real World* brought in millions of dollars in advertising **revenue** to MTV—and it demonstrated that the network was definitely ready to make a bigger break from its musical background. The unscripted, reality-based format quickly became the go-to solution for new programming, including *Road Rules*, which followed five strangers traveling around the world in 1994. "*The Real World* was the end of music as we know it on MTV," lamented founder John Lack.

Despite the changing nature of the network, MTV was becoming increasingly popular and more successful than ever. Even its music-based programming benefitted from the renewed attention from viewers. *Total Request Live*, or *TRL*, a daily **interactive** countdown show of the most popular videos hosted by Carson Daly, sparked renewed interest in music videos. And on September 9, 1999, the MTV Video Music Awards—hosted by comedian Chris Rock and featuring performances by Kid Rock, Ricky Martin, the Backstreet Boys, and Britney Spears, among others—earned a 12.9 rating, the highest in the network's history.

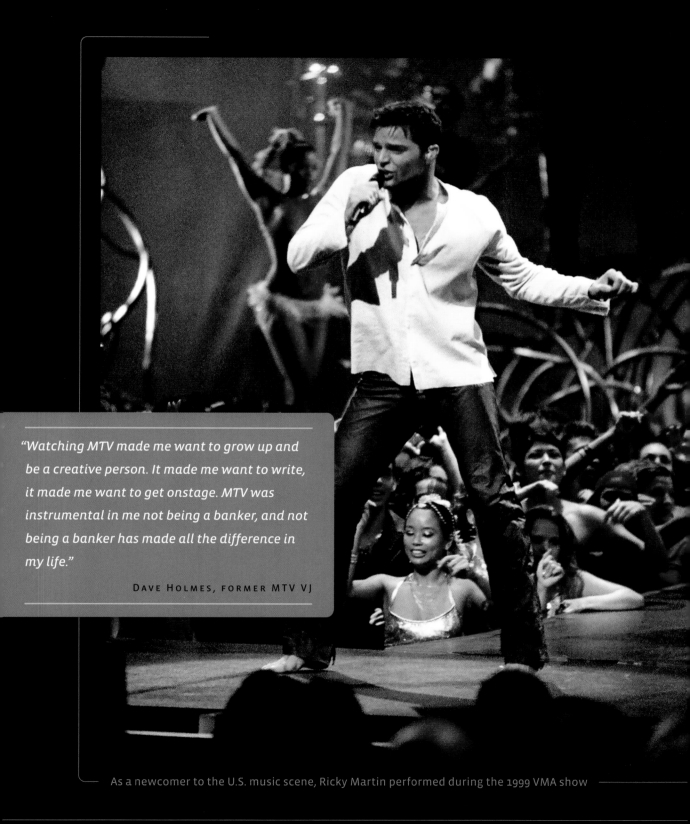

"Watching MTV made me want to grow up and be a creative person. It made me want to write, it made me want to get onstage. MTV was instrumental in me not being a banker, and not being a banker has made all the difference in my life."

DAVE HOLMES, FORMER MTV VJ

As a newcomer to the U.S. music scene, Ricky Martin performed during the 1999 VMA show

A STEP TOWARD STARDOM

Although it may be best known for helping previously undiscovered musicians become household names and for creating a new generation of reality television stars, MTV also helped launch the careers of several well-known actors and comedians. Adam Sandler, for example, cut his comedic teeth filling in for MTV VJs while he was a student at New York University; later, he was a frequent guest on *Remote Control* before being hired for *Saturday Night Live* in 1990. Another now-famous actor, Ben Stiller, was offered the role of host on *Remote Control* in 1987 but turned it down. In 1990, the *Ben Stiller Show* aired on MTV before it was picked up by the Fox cable network. And Jon Stewart, famed host of *The Daily Show* on Comedy Central, also got his start on MTV. He first appeared in the short-lived show *You Wrote It, You Watch It* before finding more success with *The Jon Stewart Show* in 1993.

Adam Sandler (right) on *Saturday Night Live*, 1993

CHAPTER FOUR

Reality Rules

The programming on MTV in 2000 included an average of only eight hours a day of music videos—a greater than 30 percent drop from the time devoted to videos just five years earlier and a 60 percent reduction from the original 24-hour commitment to the format.

"The novelty of just showing music videos has worn off," said Van Toffler, then president of MTV. "Music will remain the soul of MTV. Our non-music shows just get more press. What matters most to us is pleasing our audience."

According to the numbers, MTV was definitely accomplishing that goal. In 2001, as MTV celebrated its 20th anniversary with a 12-hour retrospective featuring more than 100 classic videos, *Billboard* magazine reported that MTV was reaching at least 77 million households, more than any of its **competitors**; VH1 was the next closest, with 74 million. And although many of those viewers were tuning in to watch such music-based shows as *Total Request Live*, many more were choosing to watch the growing number of reality shows on the network.

Although many of those shows, including the short-lived *Kathy's So-Called Reality* starring comedienne Kathy Griffin, had little to do with music, one of the most successful was built around the family of a famous heavy-metal musician:

The Red Hot Chili Peppers were among the performers at MTV's 20th-anniversary party in New York

Ozzy Osbourne, the longtime lead singer of Black Sabbath. *The Osbournes*, which premiered in 2002, followed Ozzy, his wife Sharon, and two of their children around their home. The show earned a reputation for the extraordinary amount of bleeped-out profanities and quickly became one of the most popular programs on MTV, drawing more than 4 million viewers per episode within months of its debut.

The Osbournes lasted for just four seasons and spawned several opportunities for its stars, including a talk show for Sharon Osbourne. Its success also gave rise to a new era of celebrity-based reality programming—including *Newlyweds: Nick and Jessica*, which documented the lives of newly married pop singers Nick Lachey and Jessica Simpson from 2003 until 2005, when the couple divorced.

The format was so popular—and so profitable for the network—that between 2004 and 2006, MTV released eight new reality shows. Among them were *Laguna Beach: The Real Orange County* and *The Hills*, which were billed as "reality drama series." Both featured wealthy teenagers whose opulent lifestyles and relationship woes, presented soap-opera style, captured the attention of young audiences.

By the time MTV celebrated its 25th anniversary on August 1, 2006, its programming had shifted almost entirely away from music videos. Most of the videos shown were aired only during the early morning hours or as part of *Total Request Live*. Although the anniversary was celebrated on MTV's website, where viewers could watch the first hour of programming from 1981, complete with the original commercials for Atari game systems and Jovan perfume, it was only mentioned once on-air, during that day's broadcast of *TRL*.

Although audiences seemed happy with the shift to reality-based shows, many musicians began to feel disenchanted with the channel that had once been dedicated to them. The only program that hearkened back to MTV's glory days was the annual VMA show—which had maintained both a solid television audience and a reputation for spotlighting the most popular performers

The Osbournes spotlighted its celebrity family's dysfunction, launching a new era of reality TV

of the day. But in 2007, singer Justin Timberlake, who won four of the coveted "Moonman" statuettes that were presented as awards and was named Male Artist of the Year, used the VMA stage as an opportunity to remind MTV of what he wanted to see. "Play more videos!" Timberlake demanded as he accepted one of his awards.

Despite Timberlake's impassioned plea, MTV went in the opposite direction in 2008. It launched another new reality show, this one based on **socialite** Paris Hilton's search for a new best friend. *Total Request Live* ended its 10-year run on the network on November 16 of that year with the video "... Baby One More Time," by Britney Spears. The resulting video void was designed to be filled with a new program called *FNMTV*, which would premiere videos on a weekly show and then gather instant feedback from fans through the MTV website. "Our audience has an insatiable hunger for the new and the fresh," said Amy Doyle, the senior vice president of music and talent for MTV. "We're going to be loud about what's new and use the power of MTV to engage music fans around music videos."

Besides *FNMTV*, which aired during the summer of 2008, videos were shown only in small snippets throughout the day, usually on half of the screen as the closing **credits** of a program ran on the other half. The full versions of those videos were available on the network's website, MTV.com, which had become its primary outlet for music videos. The channel had so completely abandoned its musical heritage that, in 2008, the average day of programming included just three hours of music videos.

"MTV was great for music and great for the country. Everybody watched it to get their style, to know what was hip and cool. It was a lifestyle channel."

MARTY CALLNER, MUSIC VIDEO DIRECTOR

After receiving several awards at the 2007 VMAs, Justin Timberlake won Video of the Year in 2013

A BREAK IN THE MUSIC

When terrorists flew two planes into the World Trade Center towers in New York City and another into the Pentagon in Washington, D.C. on the morning of September 11, 2001, MTV abandoned its regularly scheduled programs for the rest of the day and, like many other cable stations, devoted its coverage to the unfolding events. In place of such programs as *MTV Cribs*, *True Life*, and *The Real World*, both MTV and sister station VH1 showed footage and commentary on the disastrous event from CBS News until 11:00 P.M. that night. Although both networks stopped **simulcasting** the news then, neither returned to its usual fare. Instead they played a loop of videos over and over again, without commercials, until September 14. Regular programming resumed when a subdued Carson Daly hosted a special edition of *Total Request Live* that included discussion about the tragedy.

CHAPTER FIVE

Removing the Music

Early in 2009, MTV decided to reverse that trend by adding a six-hour block of music videos back to its schedule. *AMTV* aired from 3:00 A.M. until 9:00 A.M. every Monday through Thursday and included interviews with and performances by popular artists, along with videos. At the same time, the network brought back the *Unplugged* format, featuring such musicians as singer Adele and rapper Lil Wayne.

Although only short clips of the programs were aired on MTV itself (usually during *AMTV*), the full segments were available at MTV.com, where MTV hoped that younger viewers would find a connection with the content.

At the same time that the network appeared to be returning to its roots, it took a giant step in the other direction. In 2009, MTV introduced a trio of shows, each of which was instantly popular and controversial. The attention they garnered also effectively overshadowed the network's efforts to bring music back to its programming.

The first show, *16 and Pregnant*, debuted on June 11, 2009, and quickly became one of the most highly ranked programs on MTV (achieving the top ranking for its time slot among women between the ages of 12 and 34). The documentary-style

Teen Mom followed the girls first featured on *16 and Pregnant* as they experienced parenthood

show followed teenagers during their pregnancies in an effort to provide an honest look at what it's like to become a parent during high school. Its success led to the December launch of *Teen Mom* and then *Teen Mom 2*, both of which moved forward with the struggles of motherhood.

Although some **critics** faulted the shows for glamorizing teen pregnancy, others hailed their efforts at helping teens better grasp the consequences of their actions. In 2010, as the teen birth rate in the U.S. declined by 9 percent, the National Campaign to Prevent Teen and Unplanned Pregnancy reported that 82 percent of the teenaged viewers of *16 and Pregnant* believed the show helped them gain a better understanding of teen parenthood as well as how to avoid becoming teenaged parents themselves.

It was harder for critics to find the redeeming qualities of *Jersey Shore*, a reality show that followed the lives of eight Italian-American roommates spending their summer together in Seaside Heights, New Jersey. The first episode, which was broadcast on December 3, 2009, drew only 1.3 million viewers. But by the time the first season's **finale** aired in January 2010, 4.8 million people were hooked. *Jersey Shore* quickly became the highest-rated program in MTV's history.

Even before the show debuted, however, MTV faced harsh criticism from a number of groups, including Italian Americans who were insulted by the disrespectful terms—particularly "Guido" and "Guidettes"—that cast members used to describe each other. Several longtime MTV advertisers, including computer company Dell and pizza chain Domino's, requested that their ads not be shown during the show. And New Jersey governor Chris Christie, angered that most of the cast members were natives of New York, encouraged people to come visit the state themselves rather than watch its portrayal on TV. "I welcome them to come to New Jersey anytime," Christie said prior to the start of the second season. "The Jersey shore is a beautiful place, and it's a place that everybody should come on vacation this summer."

As *Jersey Shore* became one of the most popular shows on all of television, MTV

Jersey Shore's Paul "Pauly D" DelVecchio and Nicole "Snooki" Polizzi became overnight sensations

executives quietly made a decision that changed the identity of the network. On February 8, 2010, they unveiled a modified version of the logo that had represented the network since 1981. Although it retained the familiar block letter *M* and scribbled *TV*, it no longer had the words "Music Television" underneath them. To viewers who had been fans when the station played nothing but videos, removing those words was a confirmation that MTV had indeed abandoned the music. But to the network itself, it was a change made to connect with a new, younger audience. "The logo is part of MTV's reinvention to connect with today's millennial generation and bring them in as part of the channel," a press release statement read.

In 2011, MTV celebrated its 30th anniversary. But most of the celebration took place on its sister station, VH1, which broadcast a three-day tribute to MTV that again included the first hour of programming from 1981. On MTV itself, meanwhile, the cast members of *Jersey Shore* were completing their fifth season and negotiating for a sixth—and final—season to be aired on the network. The series ended in December 2012.

Although change has been almost constant at MTV, some elements have stood the test of time. *The Real World*, for example, has maintained its presence on the network for 20 years and continues to evolve. The VMAs attract millions of viewers each year. And recently, the network announced plans to bring back the music, albeit in a different format. The website Artists.MTV was launched in the summer of 2012 to give both established and emerging artists a way to connect with more fans. By 2013, rumors were circulating that the network might consider producing videos for musicians as well.

From its earliest days of struggling to find enough videos to fill 24 hours' worth of programming to its more recent departure from music-based programming, MTV has changed and grown along with its audience for more than 30 years. Whether it was airing videos or creating new reality shows, the network has always pushed the boundaries of conventional television—and will likely continue to do so for decades.

"I do miss when MTV played more music videos. However, it's important to be modern and change with the times."

LADY GAGA, SINGER

Popular singers such as Taylor Swift continue to use MTV and its events to reach out to fans

ON THE JERSEY SHORE

In the three short years that *Jersey Shore* ran on MTV (December 2009–December 2012), the show and its stars made a lasting mark on American popular culture. The cast members—who were hired more for their candor, honesty, and boldness than for their beauty—became household names and instant fodder for **tabloid** newspapers and magazines. Their favorite phrases were quoted by millions of television viewers across the country. One of the most popular expressions was "GTL," which was coined by stars Paul DelVecchio, also known as Pauly D, and Mike "The Situation" Sorrentino; it referred to the required elements of their days: gym, tan, laundry. At the conclusion of the show's sixth season, Sorrentino summed up its importance to American television and culture: "It will take a number of years to try to forget what we've done," he said. "We changed the way people view reality TV."

GLOSSARY

acoustic not having electrical amplification

board of directors a group of people in charge of making decisions for a publicly owned company

competitors organizations that try to get the business or attention of the same group of customers

credits a list acknowledging the contributors to a movie or television program that is scrolled down the screen at the end of the program

critics people who review literary, musical, or other artistic works and express their opinions about them

debut the first public appearance or presentation of a new product or performance

documentary a movie or a television or radio program that uses pictures and interviews with real people to provide a factual report on a topic

emerging becoming known or gaining prominence

executive a decision-making leader of a company, such as the president or chief executive officer (CEO)

finale the last episode of a television series

genre a category of music or literature defined by similarities in form, style, or subject matter

interactive allowing for a flow of information between users or viewers, and providing a means to respond to users

logo a symbol or small design used as the visual identity of an organization

market a geographic region or segment of the population to which companies try to appeal

medium a means of communicating information to the public, such as television, newspapers, radios, books, magazines, and movies

network the system for distributing television content to a group of broadcasters

producer a person who supervises the making of a musical recording, television program, or similar work

profits money that a business keeps after subtracting expenses from income

revenue the money earned by a company; another word for income

scriptwriters people who write the scripts, or texts with all the lines of dialog, for television shows and movies

simulcasting transmitting the same program or event coverage on two or more channels at the same time

socialite a person who is known for participating in social activities and entertainment events

tabloid related to sensational (or interesting but sometimes inaccurate) coverage of celebrities and popular culture

SELECTED BIBLIOGRAPHY

Anson, Robert Sam. "Birth of an MTV Nation." *Vanity Fair*, November 2000. http://www.vanityfair.com/culture /features/2000/11/mtv200011.

Hay, Carla. "Proper Role of Music TV Debated in U.S." *Billboard*, February 17, 2001.

IMDb.com. "Music Television (MTV)." http://www.imdb .com/company/co0063774/.

Marks, Craig, and Rob Tannenbaum. *I Want My MTV: The Uncensored Story of the Music Video Revolution*. New York: Dutton, 2011.

MTV.com. "MTV Timeline." http://mtvpress.com/shows /mtv_timeline.

MTV editors. *MTV Uncensored*. New York: MTV, 2001.

INDEX

A

ad campaigns 10
advertisers 8, 10, 16, 18, 26, 40
AMTV 38

B

Beavis and Butt-head 24
Billboard 6, 30
Brown, "Downtown" Julie 16
Buggles 5, 8, 21
  "Video Killed the Radio Star" 5, 8, 21

C

Callner, Marty 35
Casey, Steve 13
Choose or Lose 24
Christie, Chris 40
comedians 16, 24, 26, 29, 30
  Sandler, Adam 16, 29
  Stewart, Jon 24, 29
  Stiller, Ben 29
critics 8, 40

D

Daly, Carson 26, 37
dance shows 16
Doyle, Amy 34

E

executives 6, 8, 10, 13, 14, 18, 22, 26, 42

F

FNMTV 34

G

game shows 16, 18, 29
  Remote Control 16, 18, 29

H

Herzog, Doug 16
Holmes, Dave 27

J

Jackson, Michael 10

"Thriller" video 10

L

Lack, John 6, 8, 26

M

Masters, Lee 18
MTV
  first broadcast 5, 8, 21, 32, 42
  headquarters 8
  logo 5, 42
  naming of 13
  profits 10, 14, 32
  revenue 26
  viewership 10, 16, 26, 30, 32, 38, 40,
    42, 45
  website 32, 34, 38, 42
MTV Movie Awards 24
MTV Unplugged 22, 38
Murray, Jonathan 24
musical artists 6, 8, 10, 16, 18, 22, 26, 34,
    38, 42, 43
  Lady Gaga 43
  Spears, Britney 26, 34
  Stewart, Rod 6, 8
  Timberlake, Justin 34

N

Newman, Allen 14
news shows 16

P

Pittman, Robert 8, 13, 14
producers 14, 24
programming shifts 16, 18, 24, 26, 30,
    32, 34, 43

R

reality shows 24, 26, 30, 32, 34, 37, 38,
    40, 42, 45
  The Hills 32
  Jersey Shore 40, 42, 45
  Laguna Beach 32
  Newlyweds: Nick and Jessica 32

  The Osbournes 32
  The Real World 24, 26, 37, 42
  16 and Pregnant 38, 40
    spinoffs 40
record companies 6, 8, 10
Rhodes, Nick 19

S

Schneider, Jack 6, 10
Seibert, Fred 13
September 11 terrorist attacks 37
Sykes, John 10

T

television ratings 16, 18, 26, 40
Teller, Al 11
Toffler, Van 30
Total Request Live (TRL) 26, 30, 32, 34,
    37

V

VH1 14, 22, 30, 37, 42
Viacom 14, 16
Video Music Awards (VMAs) 10, 26, 32,
    34, 42
VJs 8, 16, 27, 29

W

Warner-Amex Satellite Entertainment
    Company 6, 8, 14

Y

Yo! MTV Raps 18
You Wrote It, You Watch It 24, 29